W9-DBT-116

WELFARE FOR THE WELL-TO-DO

by

Gordon Tullock

A Fisher Institute Publication

This edition has been produced as part of
the publishing program of The Fisher Institute.

ISBN: 0-933028-21-0 (hardback)
ISBN: 0-993028-22-9 (paperback)

Library of Congress Catalogue Number 83-80789
Printed in the United States of America

The Fisher Institute

In the business of deregulating freedom

The Fisher Institute is a non-profit, non-political public policy research organization which calls upon a great variety of economics specialists from universities throughout the world. It publishes books, papers and other materials to direct government, business and public attention toward the use of competitive markets to solve America's long-range business and economic problems.

The primary goal of the Institute is to provide useful, well-documented studies on contemporary public policy issues in language understandable to the educated consumer and business person. And, because of the independent, private nature of the Institute, its publications are also adaptable for use in school and college classrooms.

The work of the Institute is assisted by an Editorial Board which includes:

The Fisher Institute is financed by gifts, grants and receipts from the sale of its publications and services. Gifts and grants are tax exempt to donors under the provisions of Section 501 (c) (3)-1 (d) of the Internal Revenue Code.

President of the Institute
Sherrill E. Edwards

Program Director
Dr. John W. Allen

THE FISHER INSTITUTE
6350 LBJ Freeway
Suite 183E
Dallas, Texas 75240
Telephone (214) 233-1041

ABOUT THE AUTHOR

Dr. Gordon Tullock is University Distinguished Professor at George Mason University and Editorial Director of the Center for Study of Public Choice. He is past president of the Southern Economic Association and the Public Choice Society. His many books in the fields of economics and public policy include, "The Politics of Bureaucracy," "Private Wants, Public Means: An Economic Analysis of the Desirable Scope of Government," and "Modern Political Economy: An Introduction to Economics." In 1982 Dr. Tullock received the Lester T. Wilkins Award for "The Outstanding Book in the Field of Criminology and Criminal Justice" for his book, "Trials on Trial: The Pure Theory of Legal Procedures."

PREFACE

In a way, I am getting two books for the work of one. I have a scholarly book, *Economics of Income Redistribution,* which is coming out in the regularly scholarly press through Martinus Nijhoff *(Economics of Income Redistribution,* Kluwer-Nijhoff Publishing, Boston, Hingham, Mass.), and this popular version issued by The Fisher Institute. In these days of publish or perish, any other academic will recognize this as a coup.

But the point of this preface is not to point out an academic coup, but to beg tolerance of the reader. This version is intended for general consumption and not for the technically trained economist. Almost all of the technical analysis and footnotes have been left out. Anyone who might want to check a reference or who feels that my reasoning is incomplete must turn to *Economics of Income Redistribution.* Thus, if you find something incomplete here, please be charitable and look at the longer work.

Not only is the larger book condensed here, but also drastically reorganized. This book has been made easy to read for an audience which will, it is hoped, not be primarily professional economists. For some readers it may stimulate reference to *Economics of Income Redistribution,* but for most readers this is a self-contained unit which can be used by and of itself.

I thank Sherrill Edwards for his editing, The Fisher Institute of which he is president for sponsoring the entire research for *Economics of Income Redistribution,* and Norene Essary for her help in preparing this popular version.

Gordon Tullock

TABLE OF CONTENTS

Preface i

Chapters

I. Introduction 1

II. Helping the Poor 15

III. The Machiavellians and the Well-Intentioned 31

IV. Old-Age Pensions 51

V. Helping the Poor vs. Helping the Well-Organized 63

I.
Introduction

Most discussion of income redistribution revolves around the Robin Hood state. Should the government take from the rich and give to the poor or should it leave the poor to private charity? The methods used in such transfers, and statistics on the actual income distribution, etc., are also examined. These are important topics and will be dealt with in this book, albeit with a great deal less emphasis than is customary. Basically, however, those questions miss the bulk of government income and wealth redistribution. Primarily, income redistribution by the government is not taking from the rich and giving to the poor. It is taking from some members of the middle class and giving to other members of the middle class based on how well-organized they are politically.

This statement may surprise many readers and they may quite reasonably ask for some evidence. The claim here is directly contrary to much of the existing literature. The evidence will come later in the book because it is necessary to discuss a series of programs one at a time to show their actual impact. But here we can at least talk about the theory.

Most people are to some extent charitable — that is, they are willing to help people worse off than themselves — but also, the amount of aid most people are willing to give is distinctly limited. As a rough rule of thumb, few people are willing to reduce their own living standard more than 5 percent in order to help people outside their families. There are, of course, saints who are willing to give up almost everything, and there are other people who for religious reasons tithe, which may reach 16 or 17 percent among Mormons. It is not obvious, however, that these religious gifts are truly charitable even though they do help the poor. In a way, they are purchasing a particular form of fire insurance: Laying up treasures in heaven where thieves do not steal and moths do not corrupt.[1]

But if people are genuinely charitable to a small extent, they are also genuinely selfish to a large extent. People on the whole give away less than 5 percent of their income. Further, most would like to have their income larger than it is. We observe in the market a lot of people industriously, and usually ingeniously, attempting to make money. To say that they are maximizing their income is a simplification, because almost nobody works as hard as is physically possible. Strictly speaking, they are maximizing utility, and as one aspect of maximizing utility they work reasonably hard and skillfully to make money, but they also devote some time to leisure activities.

If this is the way people behave in the market, we should not be surprised to discover that they behave the same way in politics. Today the individual who works hard and thinks carefully in order to make money in the market will also work hard and think carefully in order to use the government to increase his wealth. From the individual standpoint, the effort and ingenuity he puts into the project and the return he gets are the important variables, not whether he is using the government or the market for his income.[2] Thus, we should anticipate that effort and ingenuity would be put into using the government for gain, and if we look at the real world we do indeed see such activities.

Further, in the particular case of government activity, the transfer of funds from one person to another directly injures the person from whom the money is transferred. In the market this is not necessarily true. If a new drugstore is opened, it may indeed bankrupt the old drugstore across the

[1]*Holy Bible,* St. Matt. 6:19.

[2]This is a rather general statement. There are individuals who have strong moral feelings about the use of one or the other of these two methods. Oddly enough, there are probably far more people who think it perfectly legitimate for civil servants to work hard to try and raise their civil service grade, and hence their salaries, but who think market activity is wicked, than there are of people who have the reverse feeling.

street, but by doing so confers benefit on the customers who used to go across the street and now go to the new store because the prices are lower. No doubt the other drugstore owner will be irritated, but most of the people involved in the transaction are benefited. It is easy to demonstrate, in fact, that the total benefit — that is, the benefit of the owner of the new drugstore together with the benefit of his customers — will be greater than the total injury suffered through the loss of the old drugstore.

In the government, these relationships are quite different. First, if someone succeeds in getting the government, under one pretext or another, to transfer funds to him, he alone is benefited. On the other hand, the people who pay taxes are unambiguously injured, and it is fairly easy to demonstrate that this injury in sum total is greater than the benefit.

In such a case there are additional costs. Suppose that someone would like to have a $1-per-year tax laid on 100 designated citizens of Dallas for the purpose of paying him $90 (there are some administrative costs). He should be willing to invest resources, probably in the form of lobbying congressmen, up to at least $75 to get the $100. Thus, the net gain may be as little as $15. The net cost to the victims is clearly $100. Possibly, the victims will find out about the scheme (as we shall see later, the people injured frequently do not notice the small, highly dispersed injury) and invest at least some resources trying to prevent him from getting the transfer.

It is fairly easy, then, for a transfer of this sort, in net, to cost a great deal more than the net benefit. Suppose, to make up some numbers, that it cost the beneficiary $75 to get his $90. And suppose the people who were injured by paying the $100 tax had done some lobbying which cost, let us say, $25. Under these circumstances, the net gain would be $15 and the total cost to the victims would be $125, or more than eight times the beneficiary's gain.

We will deal with this problem later in more detail. It should be pointed out here, however, that if people voluntarily make gifts to the poor this problem does not arise. Indeed, we get the reverse effect. If we give some poor man $1, presumably this gives us more satisfaction than any other use of that $1. The poor man also gets $1, so this single $1 pays off double to society as a whole.

This trick depends, of course, on the donors actually wanting to make the gift. As we shall see below, there are arguments for making such gifts collectively rather than individually, although whether these arguments are conclusive is debatable. But if the givers really want to make the gift, whether they choose collective or individual channels, we get this super-efficiency, while transfers which the donors do not want to make are highly inefficient.

We have not here counted all of the costs. In general, a simple, direct transfer of the sort described would be impossible because a simple tax of $1 would be too conspicuous. The newspapers would talk about it, the 100 voters to be injured would vote against anyone who proposed it, and it wouldn't pass. Nevertheless, we do observe a great many direct transfers in which the government is used to move money from a large group of people to a smaller group. Normally, these are not payments to the poor and, indeed, probably on the average the recipients have somewhat more money than the people making the indirect payments. How is the trick accomplished?

The answer is quite simple. There is logrolling, combined with deception and indirect methods. Unfortunately, deception and indirect methods in general add a further element of inefficiency to the whole process. Some manufacturers, for example, are somewhat indirectly given a monopoly which they can then use to charge higher prices. This is only one of many methods. We will later turn to cases in which direct cash payments are made. But for now we will confine ourselves temporarily to monopoly. All economists know that monopolies are inefficient in the sense that the cost to the people who pay the higher prices is greater than the benefit to the people who receive them. Thus, this kind of transfer is apt to be even less efficient than the direct transfers described above.

There is an even further element of inefficiency here. Normally, in order to get a monopoly through political channels, whether these channels are bureaucratic or legislative (or occasionally judicial), it is necessary to pay off various other special interest groups. As an example, I live in Blacksburg, Virginia, and normally fly out of Roanoke. For many years Piedmont Airlines was compelled to provide five seats northbound and five seats southbound every day in Pulaski, Virginia. This was an immensely inefficient operation economically, but politically the payoff to Piedmont was undeniably such that they were willing to continue the service. It was a small price to pay for their monopoly on substantially every route out of Roanoke. Still, inefficiency is high.

As we can see, there is a large element of inefficiency in these transfers, and it is depressing that the modern welfare state consists of a pastiche of such arrangements. The big items, the Social Security System for example, operate somewhat differently and we will discuss them below, but the immense collection of special legislative and administrative rules which in fact transfer funds from one part of society to another, raise all of the costs which we have listed above and confer benefits only on the people who receive the transfers. Even they do not do wonderfully well.

To make the matter more concrete, let me take an example which I am sure will be neutral to most of my readers: the British Columbia Egg Marketing Board.[3]

Some time ago the people who produced eggs in British Columbia decided that they weren't making enough money and that they had enough political power to get the government to assist them by raising the price of eggs for the consumers. Before we talk about the problems of lobbying something like this through, let me describe the ultimate out-

[3]The analysis below is based mainly on *The Egg Marketing Board,* by Thomas Borcherding, with Gary W. Dorosh, Fraser University, Vancouver, 1981.

come. Each farmer with a history of raising eggs in British Columbia has a quota of eggs which he can deliver to the Egg Marketing Board and which are the only eggs which can be sold in British Columbia. The Egg Marketing Board then sells as many of these eggs as it can to the consumers at what it determines to be a good price for fresh eggs. This price tends to be about 10 percent higher than in the United States. Since the American agricultural prices are also raised to some extent by government action, it is likely that the price of eggs in Canada is even more than 10 percent higher than the equilibrium price one could expect if there were no cartel.

This leaves the Marketing Board, however, with additional eggs. All of these eggs are sold for industrial use, such as powdered or frozen eggs. They are sold at whatever price the market will pay. Thus, for example, a bakery in Hong Kong could buy eggs from British Columbia at a lower price than the citizens of Vancouver.

The egg farmer is then paid a price which is determined by considering the percentage of eggs that go into each of these markets. For example, if 90 percent of the eggs are sold in the fresh egg market and 10 percent for industrial use, he gets a price which is calculated just as if 90 percent of his eggs had gone to the fresh market and 10 percent to the industrial market. This is well above the market he would get without the cartel but, of course, not as high a price as is paid by the consumer. In a way the consumer's high price subsidizes both the egg producer and the industrial users of the "breaker" eggs, who receive a somewhat lower price because of the increased supply of eggs for that purpose. Granted the international market in such out-of-shell egg products, it is doubtful that the price is, in fact, lowered very much. A somewhat similar arrangement for milk in the United States did sharply lower the price of milk to cheese makers.

The price of eggs being higher than the price obtained without this cartel, it is to the advantage of any egg producer to produce more eggs than he would have produced at the equilibrium price, and it's to the advantage of various other people to enter the egg business. This is dealt with by giving people the quotas mentioned above, which they cannot exceed. With this arrangement, oddly enough, the quota itself becomes the most valuable part of the egg manufacturing facility. Persons who buy egg factories in British Columbia pay considerably more for their quotas than for the physical equipment and stock of the plant.

But how did this not only inefficient but also inequitable institution get established? British Columbia is after all a democracy, and one would think that the large number of voters who have to pay higher prices for their eggs would be annoyed and the rather small collection of voters[4] who either produce eggs or are in one of the industries that uses out-of-shell eggs could be easily out-voted. If we look carefully at how democracies actually work, however, we will see why such institutions are common.

I should pause here to point out that although they are quite common in democracies, they are also quite common in dictatorships. The explanation as to why they occur in democracies should not be taken as a criticism of democracy as contrasted to what Winston Churchill called "the other forms of government which have been tried from time to time." We should do everything we can to improve democracy, but should not make the mistake of assuming the defects of democracy indicate that Caesar would be better.

The first thing to be said about such a thing as the Egg Marketing Board is that it is, in fact, rather difficult to establish. Two things are necessary: political organization on the part of the proponents and ignorance, or better yet, a state of pronounced misinformation on the part of the victims. Neither of these is easy to arrange, and it is likely that the number of market restrictions and other indirect transfers we see in the real world, large though it is, is but a small fraction of the potential number. We should all give thanks for this.

[4]There are less than 200 egg producers in the province.

Further, it is highly probable that these arrangements are hard to make originally, but once they are in existence tend to stay. The result is that over a long period of political stability a democracy develops more and more such arrangements. Indeed, Mancur Olson, in an important new book, *The Rise and Decline of Nations,*[5] suggests that this may be the basic reason for differential growth rates in modern states. Germany and Japan have grown rapidly since World War II since the catastrophe of that war wiped out the organized special interest groups, and it takes time for them to reorganize. England, Canada, United States, are growing much more slowly because we have had the good fortune to have a comparatively stable and successful government. The result is that this kind of organization has become more and more common. But this is a new theory and, it must be admitted, has not been proved.

Let us be more prosaic and simply consider the problems of organizing such an interest group. Suppose that some producer of eggs in British Columbia decides he would like to have higher prices and that political action is the appropriate way to accomplish that goal. The first thing he must do is get some other farmers to agree with him and they must all be willing to invest some resources in lobbying for their objective. Now this lobbying does not in general mean bribing legislators. It probably does involve a certain amount of rather misleading propaganda in which you tell them that the Egg Market Board is good for the country, but basically what you tell legislators is that you have votes for them if they vote for the Egg Marketing Board and against them if they vote against it.

There are two clear costs. First, there are the actual resources involved in convincing legislators that you do in fact have the votes, and in producing the misleading propaganda which will cover the operation. Second, you have to in fact produce the votes.

[5] *The Rise and Decline of Nations,* Mancur Olson, 1982. Newhaven: Yale University Press, 265 pages.

This means that the egg producers must specialize their votes. They must cast their votes in the election primarily in terms of how people stood on the Egg Marketing Board. Insofar as their votes normally would have been cast in terms of more general issues, there will be less total importance given to public interest issues. How significant this is is not clear, but it surely is a cost.

There is another important problem, first suggested by Mancur Olson.[6] Suppose I am one of the egg producers and other egg producers come to me and suggest that we set up a lobby, and that I, let us say, contribute $50 to hire professional lobbyists or produce propaganda. I will know that if I don't contribute the $50 it makes almost no difference to the lobby's likely success because I am only one of many. All of the others will know this, too, and hence everybody is likely to decide to "let George do it." Since "George" also decides to let "Dick" do it, nothing gets done.

This problem can be dealt with in a number of ways. First, there may only be a few people or corporations involved in this particular issue, with the result that the "let George do it" factor is not so important. The steel and automobile industries are examples. Second, some politician may decide to take up the issue on his own; i.e., he acts as the entrepreneur and organizer in return for the votes. As a third method, bureaucrats may take up the organizational cost, using government money, because they see an opportunity to expand the power and influence of their bureau. In practice, it is likely that the last two will occur together.

The private citizen, however, who wants to use the government to make money will be well-advised to look into the chance of organizing a pressure group and convincing some congressman or some bureaucracy that they should carry the bulk of the cost. Still, anyone organizing such a pressure group must recognize that he probably will not be able to get everyone to join, and he probably will not be able

[6] *The Logic of Collective Action,* 1965. Cambridge: Harvard University Press.

to get the people to pay in the real full value of the benefits they receive because everyone will want to let George do it.

In the only actual study of these costs that I know of, Ippolito and Mason[7] found that the cost to the milk producers of maintaining their political lobby added up to about one-quarter of their gross gain. Earlier I pointed out that people should be willing to pay much more than that, up to 85 to 90 percent of their net gain, but the "let George do it" phenomena in this case leads to there being less paid. With people being willing to put up less money, it is also likely that we have less special interest legislation.

Normally some kind of cover is necessary to conceal from voters what has happened to them. The Egg Marketing Board was argued for publicly on the grounds that it was necessary in order to retain the family farm. One of its results is that the egg marketing enterprises in British Columbia are probably inefficiently small, which also raises costs, but it is hard to argue that they are "family farms."

A second argument was that the government was protecting the consumer by stabilizing the price of eggs. It is true that eggs have varied less in Vancouver than they would without the Board, but there are a few housewives who would be happy at the exchange of a 10 percent increase in the average price of eggs for less day-to-day variation.

It will be seen that the technique involves two things: first, willingness to trade votes. The egg producers are willing to vote for people who favor the Egg Marketing Board almost regardless of what the same legislators are doing on other issues. This is an example of logrolling by the voter, and the legislator is likely to use somewhat similar techniques, trading votes more openly with his fellow legislators in order to get the bill through.

Second, the voters who are going to be injured by the act must be deceived or kept in ignorance of the matter. In the

[7]Robert A. Ippolito and Richard I. Mason, "The Social Costs of Federal Regulation of Milk," *Journal of Law and Economics,* April 1978, pp. 33-65.

case of British Columbia, the cost works out to an average of $10 a year for every family in the province, which they are not told about.

Lobbying most commonly involves minor matters which the average voter never hears of at all. The beneficiary of the rather concentrated benefit knows about it, but the widely dispersed people who are injured (all of them to a small amount) never find out about it. This is probably the kind of special interest legislation that the massive lobbying industry in Washington mainly concentrates on. Their main product is a minor change in a single clause in a bill or a bureaucratic ruling which never comes to the attention of anyone except those who will benefit.

The other case, in which people are misinformed rather than kept in ignorance, normally only covers a small collection of special interest legislation, but these are frequently the more important examples. Returning once again to the Egg Board, the average family in British Columbia probably never realizes that it is paying about $10 a year more for its eggs. For those who do realize it, however, there is the cover story of preserving the family farm and stabilizing prices. The cost is small and it would be hard for the average person to get the information necessary to evaluate these two claims. So the misinformation works for those few average voters who have the matter brought to their attention. The egg producers, a small group (under 200) whose average wealth increase is more than $300,000, have every motive to be well-informed.

But this little cautionary tale (I assure you it is quite true) is merely one small sample of an immense collection. No one, so far as I know, has actually worked out the total cost of similar situations in the United States, but is seems to me that $300 billion a year would be a modest estimate. Note that this is not budgetary cost. There are some cases in which direct payments are made; the shipping subsidies are one example. Much of our domestic farm program is another. More commonly, however, the profit comes from some kind of restriction on the competitive market which especially benefits a small group of people and the cost of which is spread thinly over a large group who won't notice.

These are typical government income redistribution activities, and they tend to be ignored in most discussions of the topic, perhaps because they are so hard to justify. Their cost to the economy is certainly much greater than the benefit to those who receive them. Further, the people who receive them, in general, have no particular merit. They get the money because they have organized themselves politically and invested resources to get it. This is profit-maximizing activity in the political realm.

The individual who is, to a large extent, working hard for his own benefit can generate large benefits for others, too, if he is operating in the right institutional environment. In the "market" for political favors, however, his drive, ingenuity, and intelligence is likely to injure others and injure others far more than the benefit he receives.

In general, this particular area of inefficiency induced by government transfers is one where professional economists like myself can perhaps take a share of the blame. It seems unlikely that most of these transfers would have gone through had public information been adequate. Professional teachers of economics should put more emphasis on explaining the real truth about these matters, both in their teaching and in their public writing. We have an opportunity to provide a considerable benefit for the public (as well as improving our own personal reputation, looking at it selfishly) by criticizing various measures of this sort when they are first presented. Most of them will not stand publicity.

But although the economists are the experts here, it is the media who bear the major blame. They, after all, have control of the channels of communication, and here is a case where they could produce large social products with relatively little investment. It is true it would have been necessary for some reporter in Vancouver to invest a half hour or so of his time to find out how things like the Egg Marketing Board have worked elsewhere, and to look at the actual plans and realize how it would work in Canada. It was, however, an easy place to improve public information with a social gain. Unfortunately, the opportunity was not exploited.

I am not criticizing any particular reporter or newspaper, or for that matter any particular economist. One individual can rarely do anything in these matters. What we need is a lot of people contributing to public information.

II.
Helping the Poor

In the last chapter we talked about a rather discouraging but important topic, the use of the government by private individuals to redistribute income for profit. In this chapter we are going to talk about a topic which is no doubt less important but which, nevertheless, is the traditional topic in the discussion of income redistribution: helping the poor. We are not going to talk only about the Robin Hood state, which takes from the rich and gives to the poor, but also about the making of gifts to the poor whether these are done by private individuals or by government.

In other words we are going to talk about transfers motivated by the desire to help other people. All of us have that desire to some extent. We are willing to make modest gifts to people who we feel are worse off than we are. We also frequently make gifts to people who we just feel we should make gifts to. The President of the United States and the Queen of England are recipients of large-scale gifts by various private persons. In both of these cases their security officials prevent them from actual benefiting from the gifts. In an unusual case, after the Kennedy assassination, Officer Tibbets' family received over $400,000 in completely unsolicited gifts from total strangers. More remarkably, Marina Oswald received $200,000 in similar gifts. It would be easy to feel sorry for either of these people — after all Mrs. Oswald was in no way responsible for her husband's crime — but it is not at all clear that they were particularly bad off. I don't know the Dallas police force arrangements for families of officers killed on duty, but I doubt that they faced any real poverty.

Note that we are not talking about intra-family gifts. That is not because intra-family gifts are unimportant; they are immensely important in both the family and the economy as a whole. They, however, do not raise any particular policy issues. We will therefore confine ourselves to gifts outside the family.

To repeat, most people do feel certain charitable urges and are willing to help people who are poorer than themselves. We will discuss this phenomena and, in particular, whether it should be done privately or collectively. In this case, however, the collective provision is somewhat unusual. When we talk about people who are motivated by charitable motives, the person who receives the charity is not an example. In other words, if we think of a democracy in which everyone can vote, which is the normal practice, we do not get an expression of pure charity but an expression of charity on the part of some people and a selfish desire to get more money on the part of the people who receive the transfers. In order to simplify the discussion we will leave that case until later. Here, we will assume that people receiving charity do not vote and any democratic voting is entirely on the part of those who are making the gift. This is, in general, not our normal procedure in the United States. Interestingly enough, it was the law in England until the end of the 19th Century, and it was in practice, although not in theory, the procedure in many parts of the United States.

As an example, let's use one obvious case in which American citizens engage democratically in making charitable gifts and in which the recipients of the charity are not permitted to vote. This is foreign aid. Foreign aid goes to people who are much poorer than the average American (at least that part of it which is not siphoned off by the higher government officials in the recipient country), but these people are not permitted to have any role in the decision process as to how much they will receive. So when we talk about democratic voting for charity in this chapter, think not in terms of the payment to poor Americans who are permitted to cast their votes and are apt to vote primarily for congressmen who want to raise that amount, but in terms of aid to poor citizens of, let us say, Bangladesh, who do not have that right to influence the decision.

Of course, not only democracies engage in helping the poor. Indeed, almost every government of which we have any historic record has done this to some extent. In fact, the evidence on the matter is weak, but apparently the poor did relatively about as well in the United States in 1850 as they do today, before we had what we call the welfare state. Incomes in general have risen, including the incomes of the poor, but individual poor persons appear to receive about the same relative share. There doesn't seem to be any data on other countries from which this comparison can be extended, but it is certainly true that aid to the poor has been part of the government agenda in most societies of which we have any record. That, of course, does not prove that government aid to the poor is desirable, and it certainly does not prove that the poor are better off with government aid than with private gifts.

Regardless of that, let us start with private gifts. As I mentioned in the last chapter, private gifts have an intriguing characteristic of super-efficiency; i.e., $1 produces $2 worth of net utility. The giver gets $1's worth of satisfaction out of his gift and the receiver also gets $1's worth. If we consider private charitable organizations as they have existed in the past and exist now, we quickly observe a phenomenon which involves limited collectivization. For example, a wealthy man will agree with his Alma Mater that he will match gifts from other people to the university. Once he has done this, if I make a gift of $1 to the university, the university in fact will get $2. I can buy gifts to the university in a cheap store.

It is not absolutely certain that this technique would lead me to give more money to the university, but it seems highly likely that it will. Note, by the way, that the wealthy man is also receiving matching utility; i.e., every dollar he gives actually benefits the university by $2. Assuming that neither I nor the wealthy man care about the other's well-being, we are each buying our charity in a low-price market by making this joint gift.

Because this technique is widely used to raise money, it appears that it actually does lead people to make larger net gifts than they would if they were not so matched. Suppose, however, that there was not just a $1-for-$1 matching as in our wealthy case, but that my $1 gift would be matched by, let us say $10 million. If I chose to give $5, $50 million would go to the poor and if I choose to give $7, $70 million. It seems likely that under these circumstances, I would choose to make a larger gift to the poor than if my $5 merely meant that the poor were better off by $5.

What has this to do with the choice between private and collective gifts? Oddly enough, Milton Friedman in his famous book, *Capitalism and Freedom,*[8] produced the first really intellectually respectable argument for government charity. Governments have been doing it for some 5,000 years without having any respectable argument, but now there is a suitable rationalization. The argument is based on the phenomena of matching given above.

Let us see how this is so. Consider the situation of an imaginary state which has 10 million citizens, all of whom are permitted to vote, and it is considering making a charitable gift to citizens of another state who, of course, do not have the vote in our first state. Each individual in a country of 10 million can, if they wish, make a gift to the citizen of the poor country. Citizens of the wealthy country might well feel, however, that they would be happier making gifts collectively, because each individual could feel that his gift was being matched by 9,999,999 others.

[8]Milton Friedman, *Capitalism and Freedom*. University of Chicago Press, Chicago, 1962.

It is not certain that they would feel this way, but it is reasonably probable. Indeed, if they have normal preferences it can be demonstrated that they would shift from the individual gift, let us say every person giving $5, to a collective gift, in which each person was taxed $7 which was then distributed. The recipients of the charity would also be better off. This argument is a strong one, but it should be kept in mind that it only applies to those polities in which the recipients of the charity are not permitted to influence the amount of the transfer. That is not the way the United States deals with its own citizens.

There are some difficulties with this demonstration, two of which I do not intend to discuss at any length. The first is simply moral principle. Most Americans feel that the government has a moral duty to help the poor, but there is a minority of Americans who feel it is morally wicked for the government to take money from its better-off citizens to help the poor. I shall let these two groups fight out the moral issue among themselves.

The second problem I will not discuss here in any detail is the difference between the model I gave above, in which the citizens directly vote on the amount they will give to citizens of another country, and the actual circumstances of our complex representative democracy. Here, I leave the subject aside not because it is uninteresting but because I have devoted much of my life to writing books and articles about the functioning of representative democracy. We can, I think, simply offer the generalization that because of the complexity of the American representative government, the majority preference is subject to a lot of random noise and disturbance in the process of being implemented. The result is that variance from the preference of a majority of the people can go either way when special interests are not involved.

Let me turn to the problems more relevant to our discussion. The first of these is the fact that the different citizens of our charitable country presumably want to give different amounts of money to the poor in the other countries. I might feel, for example, that it is desirable that everyone give $9 and you might prefer $5. The actual vote might come out with $7 per person or $70 million for society as a whole. Neither you nor I would be perfectly satisfied with this outcome.

This particular problem is inevitable in this kind of collective matching as a method of charity. Of course, it is not necessary that every individual pay the same amount. We might have a matching scheme under which the wealthy paid, let us say, twice as much as the poor, and still have everyone fairly happy. We cannot, however, adjust to individual preferences in the system.

This is clearly an objection, but it seems doubtful that discontent about the exact size of the gift on the part of individual citizens would cause them to abandon this super-efficient way of increasing the value of their gift. Given my choice of making a $9 gift to the other country or joining with the other citizens to each give a $7 gift, with the result that the country gives $70 million, I would surely select the latter.

Consider briefly this difference between a private charitable gift and a democratically-voted gift. In the case of making a private charitable gift, I know that if I give $7 or $10 to Bangladesh, it receives $7 or $10. The cost to me is also $7 to $10. On the other hand, if I vote for a tax on everyone of, let us say $7, to be distributed to Bangladesh, the cost to me is $7 and the benefit to Bangladesh is $70 million.

If I were thinking of using the private charity method, I might well assume other people would also make gifts, but the net effect of my gift would still always be exactly what it cost me, while in the democratic process that is not so.

The above argument impresses many people as paradoxical, but it can be formally demonstrated to be correct. I suppose the fact that Milton Friedman invented the argument in and of itself should be strong evidence that it is correct. He is, in the first place, an extremely competent economist and, secondly, not noted as a believer in all-encompassing state control.

The second problem I want to discuss at length is

somewhat more important. So far I have been talking about foreign aid programs in which the recipients of the charity are not permitted to vote. Transfers within the society in most democracies are not run that way. The recipients of the transfer may vote. In the United States they vote at a lower percentage than other groups, but still a great many of them do vote. Further, there is no doubt that their votes influence outcomes. Politicians do talk and vote in the legislature as if they were concerned about these recipients of transfers.

It is obvious if the recipients of charity participate in the decision as to how much charity they will receive, the givers of charity no longer are necessarily unambiguously benefited by collectivization. Instead of the givers deciding how much will be given, the givers and the receivers will jointly make the decision. Thus, the argument given above for collectivization is weakened and some would say made invalid.

Now, here we have constitutional and legal, not to say moral, problems. Surely the poor have a legal and constitutional right to vote, and most people would say they also have a moral right. I am talking here about what is desirable policy, however, not what is the current law. Further, I don't want to enter into moral debates. I will leave that problem to clergymen. Thus, I am going to confine discussion to the fact that the poor can vote on gifts to them if the gifts are made by the American government and they are American citizens. They cannot vote on gifts to them made by the American government if they are citizens of Bangladesh — as a policy question not as a question of either morals or constitutional rules. Those who feel that the moral and/or constitutional principles should take priority are quite free to debate these issues among themselves but they are not my topic.

In practice, the vote of the poor on charitable matters does not seem to make all that much difference. The actual numbers show that the poor do not do well in the United States. In 1981, the average American family of four that was completely dependent on our basic welfare program received about $4,000 in cash for the year and food stamps with a nominal value of about $2,000, for a total of $6,000 — if you regard the food stamps as having a true value equal to their nominal value, or perhaps $5,500 if you evaluate the food stamps at a lower level. Clearly, this is not an immense amount of money.

The amount received is remarkable because it is not much more than such a poor family would have received if the total amount currently being transferred by the American government as part of its many "welfare" plans had simply been divided among the whole population. I mentioned that before the development of the welfare state the poor were doing about as well as they are now. (The welfare state will be discussed at considerable length later, but I should point out now that its actual inventor was Prince Bismarck, not a man notable for a desire to help the poor. Bismarck, normally called the Iron Chancellor, is primarily known for having united Germany under the leadership of Prussia in the mid-nineteenth century. In addition, however, to his great diplomatic skills and his ability to plan wars so that he won easily, he also founded the modern welfare state. His social reforms introduced around 1880 were copied throughout the world, and our Social Security Administration and government provision of medicine are simply distant echoes of his work.)

Of course, the poor do not receive only the direct cash transfers that I have listed above. They get various government services, for example free schools, that are available to all. Most of us, however, pay taxes roughly equivalent to our receipt. That is not true with the poor because they pay relatively few taxes. Further, by a tradition going back to the Middle Ages, the poor in general receive free medical attention, currently under a combined state and federal program. Still, the total amount is by no means remarkably large.

Why the poor do not do much better than they do in a democracy in which they can vote is a little mysterious. One would think that they would receive a certain amount of money through pure charity from the people who are better off than they, and then that they could use their votes to add to that by political power. In practice, though, it looks as if they don't receive much more than they would probably receive if they were deprived of the vote. Indeed, I have on occasion argued that they would do better if they depended solely on the charitable instincts of the "better off" than they in practice do in our functioning democracy.

There are two apparent reasons why the poor do not do better than they do: one technical and one having to do with the poor themselves. To begin with the technical problem, modern government in a democracy to a large extent involves complicated bargains among different people. For example: the building of the Tombigbee Canal is traded off against a new repair contract for an anti-aircraft carrier in Philadelphia and the expansion of the wilderness areas in Idaho. The poor have a technical disadvantage in these bargains because it is obvious exactly how much they benefit from any increase in payments to them. It is not obvious how much the citizens living along the Tombigbee benefit from the construction of that canal. Thus, in the bargaining, the poor aren't able to keep any of their cards covered, whereas the people they are dealing with have almost all of them covered. Under the circumstances, it is not surprising that the poor do badly.

This technical problem is severely reinforced by the simple fact that the poor are normally poor because they lack the necessary characteristics to be well-off. Some of them are ill, which makes it difficult for them to keep their jobs and also makes it difficult for them to engage in political maneuvering. Others are not very bright which, once again, makes it difficult for them to get jobs or engage in political maneuvering. A third group lack motivation, possibly because of the absence of suitable role models, which is such a fashionable topic at the moment. This handicaps them in making a living, and also handicaps them in politics. A fourth, and in my opinion small group of the poor, are intelligent and reasonably strongly motivated, but their motives lead them to play a role in society which is not highly rewarded. This fourth group, of whom some artists are examples, normally are not motivated to become active in politics.

Thus, the poor are, in general, a group of people who don't do well in any aspect of life. The artists may do well in what interests them, but they are not likely to be effective outside that narrow sphere.

So, just as they are poor because they lack the role models, intelligence and drive necessary to make a decent income, they are also handicapped equivalently in doing well in politics. They have failed in the economic market, which is what we mean by saying that they are poor. There is no reason to believe that they will succeed in the political market. We should not be surprised that they are not able to get a high return on their votes.

Now all of this sounds like an unkind thing to say about the poor, and certainly it is not praising them, but we should not regard this as meaning that they are to be discriminated against or punished. We feel charitable motives to help those who are worse off than we are. Normally, the reason that they are worse off is irrelevant.

To summarize, there is a quite good argument for collectivizing charitable distribution when the distribution is to somebody like the citizens of a foreign country who can't vote in American elections. The argument deteriorates if we turn to the actual situation in the United States in which the recipients of charity, the poor, can vote and their vote influences how much they receive. Looking at the matter realistically, however, it does not appear that they are able to get much of a return on their vote and hence may not make much difference. It is certainly true that the genuine poor in the United States do not benefit much from the various programs which have been enacted in their name.

It may well be that the low return the poor get in the United States is simply what the voters want. The whole welfare state system may, in fact, exist not to help the poor but to make transfers to more politically influential people in the middle class, while the discussion of the poor is to a large extent camouflage. This cannot, of course, be proved and in fact may be an unjust statement. The politically influential people who get so much out of Congress may honestly be in favor of helping the poor but primarily are concerned with other matters. Certainly there is some transfer of funds to the poor.

As an example of public policy advocated to a large extent by labor unions and people who normally would refer to themselves as representatives of the lower classes, consider the "voluntary" quotas on Japanese automobile imports. Beneficiaries of these quotas, so far as they have beneficiaries, are primarily the employees of the automobile industry, who are among the most highly paid workers in the United States, and the owners of stock in the automobile companies. The stockholders are a rather more diverse group, income-wise, than the employee. Indeed, the employees by way of their pension trusts hold a good deal of stock. Nevertheless, it does not seem likely that many poor people will benefit because of the improved values of automobile company stock.

The poor people, in fact, will be injured. It should not be forgotten that the United States is a very wealthy country and many of the people we classify as poor own cars. That is particularly true in rural areas. These cars are basically secondhand cars rather than new ones, but nevertheless a rise in the price of new cars tends to "trickle down" to the purchasers of used cars.

But the quota has not actually raised the price of all cars in the United States, only some cars. The Japanese automobile industry is not managed by stupid and inept people. Being compelled to restrict the total number of cars they can ship to the United States by these quotas, they realized they could make more money on each car if they shipped in expensive cars instead of cheap cars. In consequence, they have increased their shipments to the United States of the more expensive car and reduced their shipments of the cheaper kind. The result is that the more expensive cars in the

United States aren't quite as much more expensive as they used to be. In other words, the producers of the higher priced American lines face stronger competition from Japanese companies, whereas producers of lower priced lines face much less competition. Of course, the industry as a whole faced less competition before because the total number of cars entering is restricted, but there has been a distortion of the Japanese car exports to the United States in such a way as to benefit upper income purchasers of new cars.

Now I don't want to argue here that the people who pushed this program through, presumably all of them in the top half of the income distribution, were consciously trying to injure the poor. It was just that the issue's effect on the poor was of less interest to them than its effect on their own well-being. A significant redistribution was enacted by government regulation in this case rather than by tax. The beneficiaries were automobile workers, owners of stock in automobiles, and people who buy expensive new cars. The losers were people who buy cheap new cars and, secondarily, the people who buy used cars.

This situation is not atypical. Lip service is paid to helping the poor and, of course, we in fact do help the poor a good deal, but the really big transfers made by the American government do not go to the poor. A tax on the rich and allegations that we should take money away from them, which I think come very largely from a feeling of envy, are also common. As a matter of fact, the total income by people in "the $200,000 to $500,000 bracket" is small enough that even if we could confiscate all of it, the effect on the budget would be insignificant.

The income transfer system in the United States is very largely a transfer from one group of middle class citizens to another. We do help the poor to some extent, and we do to some extent take money away from the wealthy, but both of these are minor phenomenon compared to the transfers within the middle class.

But I cannot leave the problem of helping the poor without turning to another essentially economic problem. This is well summarized in the current issue of *Public Interest:*[9]

> ". . . (I)ndividuals certainly do have an interest in work if they have no other way to support themselves or if they can make much more by working than not. Once social programs exist, however, those meeting the eligibility rules have an alternative to work. And if they are low-skilled, they are unlikely to make much more by working than by going on relief . . ."

In other words, this is the problem which the common man refers to as the welfare loafer. So far as I know, no one desires that people be permitted to draw relief in idleness, although there are, of course, some people who for physical reasons simply cannot work.

As a result of the general feeling that people should not be left idle while they are on relief, most of these programs have some kind of arrangements under which the people are required to work. To quote the current issue of *Public Interest*[10] again:

> ". . . In fact, the requirements are not effectively enforced and few recipients take them seriously . . ."

The problem here is a real one, although I do not think the current welfare administrations make any serious effort to actually enforce the working rules. Still, if they did it would be difficult. Consider the problems which someone attempting to get the unemployed to work faces. First, the number of "jobs" that you require vary sharply from day to day, depending on how many people happen to have lost or

[9]Lawrence M. Mead, "Social Programs and Social Obligations," *The Public Interest,* No. 69, Fall 1982, p. 28. New York: National Affairs, Inc.
[10]*Ibid.,* p. 22.

found jobs. Further, we would like to have them vary even from hour to hour because we would like to have it possible for someone on relief to take off at any time to investigate a job opening.

Secondly, the jobs, of necessity, must be low-skilled. That is not because there are not highly skilled people who become unemployed, but because it is unlikely that their skills will exactly fit the particular jobs available and, hence, they will have to be given unskilled jobs outside their specialty instead of skilled jobs in their specialty while on relief.

These requirements mean that the jobs we give to the unemployed must be ones in which capital investment is low and which are easy to supervise, because we cannot afford to keep immense amounts of capital and supervisory capacity available for the maximum number of unemployed we expect to be helping. Further, supervision is of necessity a little difficult here because you have to be willing to say to someone who asks for relief, "You take that rather dirty, low-paid job which we have provided for you, or you and your children will starve." Most people, and certainly most welfare supervisors, don't want to do that.

The outcome of all of this is that we can provide work for the unemployed who meet all these requirements, but probably they will not be very productive jobs. Indeed, some people writing on this subject have suggested providing completely make-work activity of the sort that involves, let us say, turning a crank against a resistance for eight hours a day. The purpose is not to produce anything but to make certain that people do not receive money in idleness. I think we could do better than that, but it would be true that we could not expect high productivity from the people on relief. Rubbish removal and picking up litter impress me as areas which meet our requirements. A man who spends his day walking 20 miles along one side of a freeway picking up litter probably will not contribute much to the national product, but at least he will not find that he is getting relief money along with a day's leisure.

If my suggestion is taken, we will provide a number of unskilled, fairly strenuous jobs for all people on relief who are physically capable of working. Then not only will the number of people interested in relief payments fall sharply but, as a matter of fact, we can raise the amount we pay them. As I mentioned above, $6,000 a year is the current average payment to a family of four in the United States. One of the advantages of this system, believe it or not, is that you can afford to be more generous. Six thousand dollars a year, with leisure, (and we must remember that leisure can be partially filled with various productive activities which can be concealed from the relief administration), is probably no more attractive than, let us say, $8,000 or $9,000 combined with a fairly strenuous, not very productive job. Thus, by putting a work requirement in, even if the work requirement does not involve much addition to G.N.P., we make it possible to increase the amount of money available to people who truly need it without attracting a bunch of welfare loafers.

III.
The Machiavellians and the Well-Intentioned

This chapter is devoted to a topic which many of my readers may think is a complete waste of time. I propose to demonstrate that programs which are designed with a means test, i.e., in which the money goes only to the poor, benefit the poor more than the Bismarckian programs in which the payment goes to substantially everyone. If the reader feels that this is obvious, he is free to skip the chapter, but I believe this discussion is necessary because there is a great deal of literature which argues the contrary.

When I first studied this subject, almost all government aid to the poor was administered only to the poor, and there was a means test to see to it that no one got welfare who wasn't poor. The generosity of the means test can perhaps be criticized. At that time, in the mid-part of the New Deal, proposals to extend them generally following Bismarck — e.g., making such things as aid to the old and the sick apply to all old and sick, not just the poor ones — were much canvassed. The standard argument was essentially one of being nice to people.

It was argued that the poor would feel insulted if you compelled them to prove they were poor. If the program were generalized, offered to everyone, then the poor would not have to prove that they were indeed poor. To make this argument a little more intelligible for modern readers, I should point out that at that time only a small portion of the population actually filled out an income tax form. Today, when almost anybody with an income is compelled to reveal that income to government officials, the argument would not appear to have much validity.

In any case, the argument is an example of Hamlet without the Prince of Denmark. The poor may indeed regret having to prove they are poor in order to receive, let us say, an old-age pension, but the person who is really not poor and who hence does not receive an old-age pension is much more likely to be benefited by the abolition of the means test than is the poor person. This argument will be worked out in more detail later in the chapter but, once again, it seems to me fairly obvious and I regret indeed having to go through the details of the argument. It is only the existing state of the literature in this area which makes it necessary for me to do so.

Today, fashionable proponents of generalizing government income transfer programs, free medicine, old-age pensions, etc., instead of confining them to the poor use another argument. This argument is that the middle class will in fact not vote enough money to provide, let us say, good medical attention to the poor if the poor are the only recipients of government medical attention. If, on the other hand, everyone receives government medical attention, the middle class will vote enough money to provide good medical attention because middle classers want it themselves, and the poor will benefit from it.

This argument is what I call well-intentioned Machiavellianism. It is argued, in essence, that we must fool the middle class into providing better medical attention for the poor by connecting it to better medical attention for the middle class itself. Personally, I do not believe that the middle class is so stupid that this trick will work. If people do not want to help the poor, they have many ways to avoid it.

In practice, complicated government programs such as free medical aid or free old-age pensions which are distributed to everyone normally involve a certain amount of filling out of forms and dealing with the bureaucracy, and the middle class is better at that than the poor. All of the statistics on the point indicate that, as a matter of fact, middle classers are more successful in getting good medical attention and schools out of the government than are the poor, even when the program is nominally open to everyone. This should not surprise us. Once again, the poor in general are poor because they are not terribly competent in various things, and dealing with the government is one of them. A man who is capable of making $35,000 a year at some private occupation is far more likely to be successful in negotiating with a bureaucrat than is the man whose earned income is $5,000 a year.

There is another problem. If we are attempting to fool the middle class into voting more money for the poor than it really wants to by attaching aid for the poor to a program which directly benefits the middle class, we should keep in mind that we are not necessarily the only Machiavellians around. I do not doubt that there are well-intentioned people who are interested in reaching good ends by rather dishonest means. Indeed, one can find many such types scattered throughout history. But although such people do exist, there are far more people who find it desirable to cover essentially selfish goals under slogans of public good, such as aiding the poor.

The Machiavellian, in this case the man who proposes generalizing government aid and claims the reason is that he wants to help the poor, and who thinks that the middle class will vote more for them if it is also on the same program, must realize that he is putting a low evaluation on the charitable desires of the middle class. He is also assuming its members aren't very bright.

He may be right about both of these things, but we should always keep in mind that he may also be wrong. Further, many of the people who argue this way may have quite selfish motives. They may be bureaucrats (or people who would like to be bureaucrats) simply interested in expanding the program so that there will be more high-ranking positions. They may be middle class types themselves, whose real concern is that they think it is unfair for the poor to receive "benefits" which they do not. In my private discussions I've found that advocates of generalizing our current medical program to cover everyone usually start by talking about the desirability of benefiting people whose income is above the present cut-off point but below their own, which indicates they are trying to benefit some people who aren't poor. Normally, however, they then go on to talk about their own situation and remark about how unfair it is that they would have to pay themselves if some kind of catastrophic illness not covered by their current insurance strikes them.

In dealing with these people I cannot say I have been effective. Aid to the poor, in my mind, raises quite different problems than providing general medical attention to everyone. The particular argument that the upper income groups are not protected against catastrophic illness is normally true, but insurance covering such illness is available, albeit expensive. There is, however, no reason why it will be cheaper if provided by the government than if provided privately. Somehow, though, I never succeed in making these points convincing.

There is here, however, another and more important point, which is that as a matter of fact catastrophic illnesses which do strike people normally are dealt with by the public sector in any event. Characteristically, if someone contracts a disease which requires hospitalization and which leaves him unable to earn an income for many years, he or his family first deplete their own resources and then turn him over to the state, which maintains specialized hospitals for this purpose. I do not wish to argue that these hospitals are particularly well-run or luxurious, but they apparently do represent the popular view of what should be done with such cases, and certainly they are not private. Only the wealthy deal with those members of their family who have catastrophic diseases through the private marketplace. Most of us do, in fact, turn to special state programs for such diseases. Once again, I have never been successful in pressing this point on people who are interested in general public medical care.

Now it may be that my inability to succeed with these arguments indicates that I am not good at disputation or that the arguments themselves are basically poor. I do not believe so. I think the reason I am unable to convince people in these areas is that they believe that whether they receive aid under these programs or not does not much effect their tax payments. In other words, they are hoping to transfer expenses to other people. They are not charitably trying to generalize, but are attempting to obtain a private profit out of government. My arguments do not have much effect because they are addressed to the overt arguments used by my interlocutors and not to their actual motives. But here again, I may be totally wrong. I am in essence implying a Machiavellian approach to the argument to the people I talk to, and this may be erroneous.

There is, however, one very clear-cut characteristic of this type of well-intentioned Machiavellianism, and that is that it is necessary for proponents to use arguments which are not their real arguments. They hope to get the bulk of the people to vote for something they don't really want — for example, greater medical attention for the poor, by attaching it to greater medical attention for themselves. The trick requires deception and it is by no means obvious that the well-intentioned Machiavellian will be the only person attempting to deceive. And in a way the well-intentioned Machiavellian is at a disadvantage compared to the more conventional Machiavellian who is not attempting to achieve a charitable goal.

Thus, we probably have alliances between well-intentioned people who are attempting to do good by deceiving the average voter and the people who are not particularly well-intentioned who are attempting to benefit by the same deception. Further, in this case it is not clear what the average voter's position is. If the average voter, for example, is interested in benefiting himself and doesn't care much about the poor, I propose to demonstrate a little later in this chapter that generalizing the means-tested program to cover the entire population is indeed an effective method of achieving that selfish objective. If you feel it is necessary to continuously talk about helping the poor but don't really care about them, you should in general be in favor of generalized programs. If you are seriously interested in helping the poor then you would want to generalize the program only if you were convinced that the majority of the people didn't feel that way and you could trick them by generalization.[11] This is, I think, unlikely, but in any event you would find yourself aligning with the genuine Machiavellians and you would not be able to tell them from the well-intentioned Machiavellians.

Once we go in for political trickery, we may well accomplish things that we could not accomplish without that trickery, but we may also be tricked. The con men say you can't cheat an honest man. I do not think that is entirely true, but it is certainly true that the man engaged in a devious plot is frequently misled, with the result that the devious plot produces something that was no part of his intention.

Let me discuss two examples. In England, the institution of the National Health Service generalized what had previously been a rather elaborate free medical service for the poor into a medical service for everyone. It happened to occur at the same time as the antibiotic revolution, the greatest medical advance in history. In spite of this tremendous improvement in medical technology, the death rate of the poorest fifth of the English population actually rose at that time. The apparent explanation is fairly simple and straightforward. There was a shift of medical resources from the poor to the middle class and the poor suffered from it.

[11]There is another argument sometimes used here which is that the poor do not know the present programs and, hence, do not apply for them, whereas with generalized programs they would be well-informed and would apply for them. I don't believe this is a truthful statement about the information status of the poor, but if it is, surely this is the most expensive conceivable kind of advertising program.

My second example comes from the United States. The passage of the medicare-medicaid programs did two things. They somewhat expanded and improved the medical aid to the poor. It should be said that this is a normal routine. We do not normally keep our various charitable programs at a continuously rising level as society gets wealthier. There are periods in which it remains stable, then a sharp rise occurs, and then another period of stability and a sharp rise. It goes up in steps. One of these steps in medical aid to the poor occurred at this time.

The other thing that happened was the extension of free medical care to all the old, not just the poor old who had had it before. The net result of the change was, of course, a sharp increase in the incomes of doctors,[12] an increase which I suppose with time will eventually disappear but is still having its effects, and a sharp increase in the well-being of older people who had enough money that they were not eligible for means-tested free medical attention. The poor whose medical attention increased did, of course, gain to some extent, but it is almost certain that the additional subsidy to older people who were not poor caused for a period a switch of medical resources away from the older poor towards these older well-off people.

Of course, those citizens of the United States who were neither old nor poor also suffered a reduction in medical attention because of the increased resources available for the older non-poor. The cost clearly fell, to a large extent, on the non-old non-poor. Whether the poor, old or young, gained or lost from the whole thing is not clear. I would say that they gained but not as much as they would have gained had the upward step not also been extended to the older non-poor. The gainers clearly were the old non-poor and the doctors.

[12] It is intriguing that the free medical attention used to be a direct charity by the doctors themselves who did not charge for poor patients. They have now succeeded in getting the government to cover this expenditure, in fact cover it with very good fees. The benefit to the doctors is probably greater than the benefit to the poor although it is likely that medical attention for the poor has also improved.

This is the kind of result that one rather anticipates from well-intentioned Machiavellians. The well-intentioned Machiavellian, in order to conceal his actual plans from the potential victims, has to refrain from public discussion of his real motives and plans. Since he has to refrain from talking about his actual motives and plans in public, he does not get the benefit of public discussion in drawing them up and may well end up as he did in this case, primarily benfiting a group of people who were most assuredly not poor.

Let us now turn to a little more formal analysis and for this purpose I will have to use some diagrams. Let me assure the reader who is unaccustomed to economics that these diagrams are simple and easy to follow. For the more sophisticated who find these perhaps too simple, a more conventional set of diagrams may be found in my *Economics of Income Redistribution*.

On Fig. 1, on the vertical axis, I show a simple dollar measure and on the horizontal axis people are arranged from left to right according to income. People who have no income at all, except government aid of some sort, are at .0, and I have rather arbitrarily stopped the table at $100,000 on the right, but there is no intrinsic reason that the diagram could not be continued out to any income desired.

Fig. 1

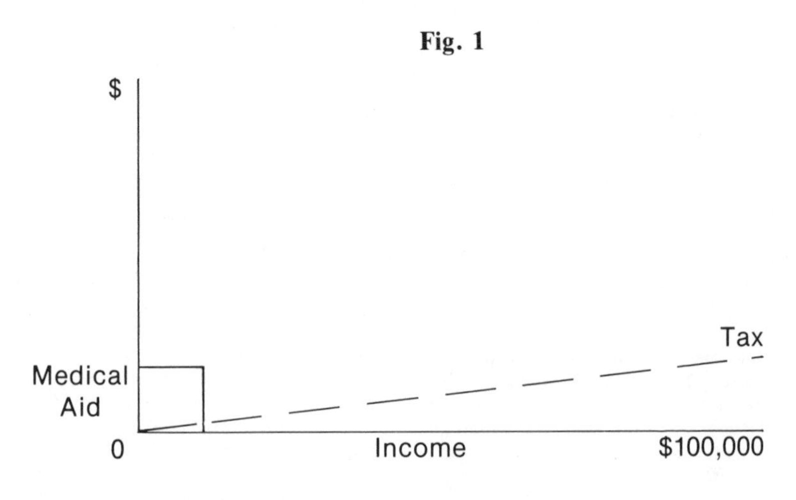

I assume that there is already in existence a government-sponsored aid program for medicine for the poor. This program, of course, like all medical aid, actually aids different people to a different degree but this, over large numbers, works out to so much per head. If the reader wishes, he can assume that the government simply gives each poor person a medical insurance policy and this policy cost is shown by the solid line marked "medical aid." I assume that this is available only to the poor, which we will assume is roughly the bottom 10 percent of the population, so that all poor people receive the aid marked "medical aid" and this drops to zero as you get beyond the level of poverty.

In general this last assumption is not true of means-tested American aid programs. As a general rule, instead of dropping off abruptly at some point they fall off gradually as incomes rise. Adjusting my diagram to take care of this gradual change instead of the abrupt cut-off at a given income makes it more complicated but does not change the principle. Once again, if the reader is interested in the more accurate representation of the present system, he will find it in *Economics of Income Redistribution,* but I can assure him that it makes no difference in principle, only in the details.

This medical aid, since it is government provided, must of course be paid for in taxes and I have assumed that the taxes rise as income rises, with people with low income paying some taxes, which they do, and people with higher incomes paying higher taxes. For simplicity in drafting a straight line is used to indicate this increase, but once again there is nothing in the reasoning that follows which requires a straight line. If the reader is interested, he can draw various other shapes, providing only that they continue to rise as income goes up.

How does this leave various citizens? The answer is shown in Figure 2. The solid line in Figure 2 is the net outcome for any citizen of the combination of the aid, if he is eligible for it, and the taxes for whom everyone is eligible. The poor person now receives his insurance policy paid for by the government but also pays in taxes, with these taxes increasing as he becomes less poor. Hence, instead of having a straight line for medical aid, this net aid (medical aid minus tax cost) slants downward slightly. As soon as one passes the point where the means test cuts off the medical aid, he, of course, receives no more medical aid but continues to pay taxes. Hence, the citizens who are well-off enough to fail the means test have a net loss on the project, shown by the line slanting downward below zero, indicating that as you get wealthier the program inflicts greater cost on you.

Fig. 2

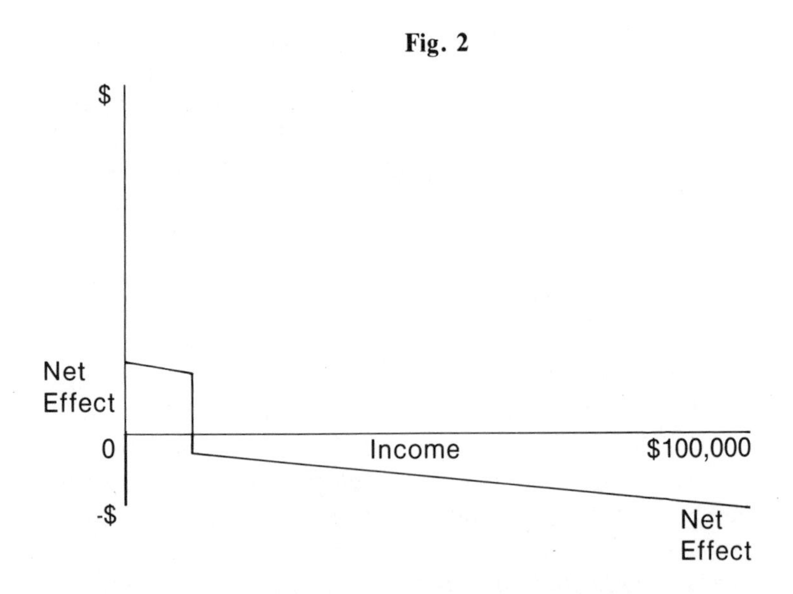

It is not obvious from the fact that the upper income people face a net cost in monetary terms that they would be unhappy about the program. They might have genuinely charitable feelings and be interested in helping the poor through the program. The line does not show their utility, but the objectively calculated tax cost to them. In fact, Figure 2 is simply calculated by subtracting the dashed tax line of Figure 1 from medical aid, with medical aid for those people who flunked the means test of course having a zero value.

On Figure 3, we show a universal medical program which provides for each citizen the same medical insurance policy, once again shown by the medical aid line but, of course, going all the way to the right. As pointed out above, this is a little unrealistic because when the government does provide medical aid and assistance, upper income people do somewhat better than lower income people, but we will leave that out here. Further, this diagram doesn't really deal with the argument that if you give the middle class free medical aid it will vote for more medical aid and, hence, benefit the poor indirectly. In this case the middle class is voting for the same amount of medical aid. We will deal with the well-intentioned Machiavellian argument below.

Fig. 3

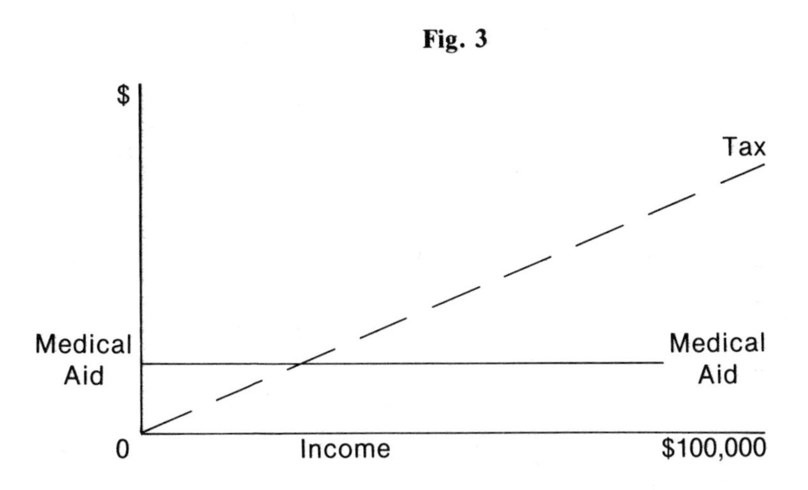

There are two differences between Figure 1 and Figure 3. The first is that medical aid is now universal and the second is that the tax is now higher. Once again, in Figure 4 we show the net effect. It will be noted that the poor receive the same medical attention they did before but pay higher taxes. A number of people who had not received free medical attention before but now receive it will pay high taxes. For some of them this is a good bargain, but for some the increase in taxes is more than the improved medical aid. In any event, the very wealthy probably will not take advantage of the government's free medical aid. From their standpoint the only effect is the increase in taxes.

Fig. 4

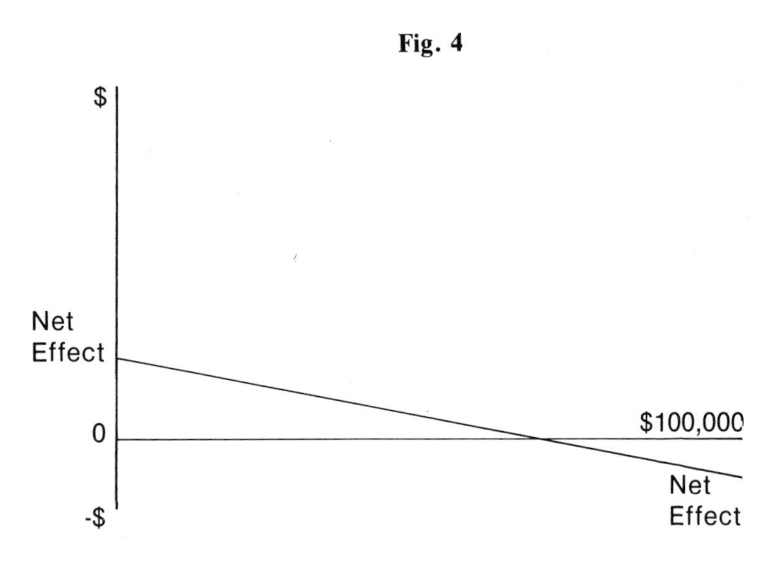

Figure 5 shows the difference between the effect on different parts of the population as shown in Figure 2 and in Figure 4. I should add that these diagrams are not geometrically completely accurate. One of the problems of drawing diagrams of this sort is that it is essential that they be intelligible, i.e., that you don't put the lines too close together. The problem can be eliminated by using algebra instead of diagrams but the diagrams are simpler. Even though they are not exactly to scale, they are not in any way misleading. Some of the effects are smaller than shown on the diagram. The diagram shows them larger simply because if I made them small enough the printer would find two lines running together.

In any event, it is clear that the universalization of the program has hurt the poor, benefited a large group of people called the middle class, and then injured the very well-off.

The reason for this is simple. Members of the middle class now receive free medical attention and, although their taxes have gone up, the tax increase is less than the value of the medical attention. The poor are receiving the same medical attention they received before but are now paying more taxes. The wealthy are paying taxes which are higher than the medical aid they now receive.

Fig. 5

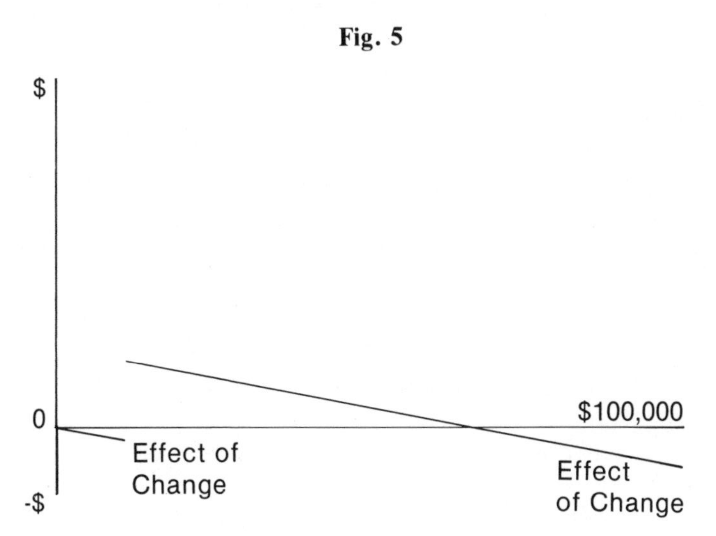

Here we see the basic problem with the Machiavellian approach to these matters. There is a large group of people who have a perfectly sound selfish reason for wanting the program to be universalized. This group of people in general is not only much larger than the poor but also politically better organized. That they favor the change is not surprising.

The Machiavellian has to believe that the people who accept the change, which in its present form will actually injure the poor, will now proceed to vote higher taxes upon themselves, thus increasing their own medical aid, and as a by-product aid the poor more than the increase in taxes which universalization of the program brought about. This, of course, is possible.

But suppose that the middle class types who in fact gain by the program are not easily fooled. There is nothing to prevent them from maintaining the previous government aid program at the level it was before, when it was aid for the poor only, and also providing that people who wish can also purchase additional services. From the middle class standpoint, if they do not really want to increase aid to the poor, this would be more efficient. As a matter of fact, all medical systems which are purportedly universal do have this characteristic although in some cases, for example Sweden and Russia, there is a little concealment of the phenomena.

Members of the middle class can, however, actually gain. They can provide exactly the same medical aid for everyone that they provided before for the poor and supplement that aid out of their own pockets for their own benefit. The result will be a small but real transfer of funds from the poor to the middle class because the poor's taxes have gone up. The universalization of medical attention is certain to transfer some money from the wealthy to the middle class. It will also transfer some funds from the poor to the middle class. Only if the universalization is combined with a rise in the level of medical aid can the poor gain. Even then the poor can be injured if the increase in aid is largely concentrated in areas which are politically influential — for example, in the suburbs rather than the central cities.

As mentioned before, in England the generalization of medical care led to an actual rise in the death rate of the poor. To be considered here is the probable phenomenon that will occur whenever you generalize aid. It should be noted that it is essentially a temporary development, not permanent. Still, "temporary" in this case may mean 20 years. What happens is fairly simple.

Let us take England in the 1930s. The wealthy could well afford excellent medical care and got it. The poor benefited from an elaborate government sponsored program of free medical aid. The middle class had to pay for its own medical attention and consequently economized on it. By this, I do not mean that its members ran serious medical risks but merely that they calculated the desirability of a doctor's visit against the desirability of some other expenditure in their budgets.

With the generalization of medical aid to all persons, the middle class now got its medical attention free and increased the amount of medical attention it received. Consumers characteristically increase consumption of goods when the price goes down.

The total number of doctors, hospitals, etc., in England, however, was the same the day after the generalization of the program as it had been before. The middle class individuals with their larger demand were able to divert a good deal of medical attention from the poor to themselves because of their greater ability to handle forms and because the doctors in practice preferred to deal with them rather than the poor since there was no monetary difference. Thus, the death rate among the poor actually rose at the time the medical service was universalized.

This was an extreme example of the injury of the poor by the generalization of the free medical attention they were already using, but something milder can be expected in every other such extension. General government-run medical programs are not a good way of helping the poor. If you are convinced that the middle class will not vote enough money to give the poor adequate medical attention, the Machiavellian technique of generalizing medical attention so that the middle class also gets it, with the objective of helping the poor, is unwise. There may be other reasons for universal medical provision by the government.

Suppose, however, that we do want to have universal medical provision by the government, and we do not want to hurt the poor who already receive such free medical attention. The universalization of the program will increase the demand for medicine by the middle class and a certain amount of medical resources will likely be transferred from the poor who have not increased their demand to the middle class, with the result that the poor get not only higher taxes but poorer medical attention. Is there anything that we can do about this?

Yes. There is a program which could be put into effect which would prevent the poor from being injured by the universalization of the program. I am going to describe such a program here. My reason for describing it is not that I wish to urge its adoption but to point out that none of the people who advocate generalization of medical care have ever talked about the matter and certainly have not made any effort to solve the problem. From this I deduce that the well-intentioned Machiavellians who actually are attempting to help the poor by this indirect means are outnumbered by the true Machiavellians in the middle class who will themselves gain by the program and who are not particularly concerned about the poor.

If we want to help the poor, there are two basic problems: the increased tax burden on the poor, which is pretty much unavoidable because general taxes do hit them even if not hard, and the fact that they would now have a smaller part of the total medical demand than they had before. These problems can be counterbalanced by another means-tested program. Under such a program, the poor not only receive the general program for the country as a whole, but receive an additional means-tested program. The purpose of it is (a) to compensate them for the increased taxes, and (b) see to it that their relative demand for medical services remains as high as it was before. In other words, in the past they received free medical services and the middle class paid the bill. Since the middle class is now receiving free medical service and, hence, are in a position to pull services away from the poor, the poor should be given some additional resources to offset that pull.

This program sounds and is bizarre. But to universalize medical attention and not injure the poor, something like this is necessary. The well-intentioned Machiavellians should be in favor of it and, indeed, it is a test to tell the well-intentioned from the not-so-well-intentioned.

Such a program could be put on a more or less temporary basis. A crash program could be introduced at the same time to increase total medical resources in society so that the total amount of resources would rise enough to compensate for the increased demand from the middle class. It would probably still be true that the middle class members would do better than the poor because of their superior ability to handle forms and bureaucrats, but with a combination of my temporary and rather bizarre program and a long-run increase in resources, the poor could still be guaranteed the same medical treatment as they had before.

As a matter of fact, no programs of either of these types have been tried by those countries which have universalized medical attention. What normally happens is, first, the incomes of doctors go up sharply because of the increase in demand, and there is a shift of resources away from the poor. Secondly, the state becomes concerned about its high expenses and begins to take advantage of its monopsony power to force the returns of doctors down. The end product is, in England, that the total amount of resources used for treatment of illness is much lower as a percentage of G.N.P. than in the United States, and you have the immense delays before medical treatment, which have excited so much comment. Indeed, private medical insurance has developed in England for people who want to get high quality and immediate medical service instead of having to depend on the state system.

But, to emphasize, all of this should not be taken as a conclusive argument against something like the British Health Plan. I am personally opposed to such a program, but I realize that there are arguments for it other than helping the poor. The fact that it is unlikely to help the poor is not a conclusive argument against it because it does not deal with the other possible reasons for establishing such a program. I would be willing to debate the issue on those other grounds, but not here.

In the discussion of a universal medical program in the United States, none of its proponents have dealt at all with the problems it is likely to inflict on the poor. The argument that it will benefit the poor is frequently made, but the reasons given are the ones that I believe I have discounted earlier in the chapter.

For purely selfish reasons, people in certain income brackets should favor it — in those brackets where they are now not eligible for free medical aid but where the taxes they would have to pay if the medical aid were made universal would be less than the benefit of the medical aid to them. Once again, this is a purely selfish drive and as far as I can see the basic support for universalization of medical service comes from that group together with certain political and bureaucratic entities in which the expansion would increase employment opportunities. In a democracy we expect people will, to a large extent, vote for those things which will benefit them. If everyone votes for things that benefit himself, then things that benefit the majority will get through. This is surely not a bad thing. But to say that this program is actually aimed at benefiting a specific group of non-poor people, a very large group, is quite different from saying that it will help the poor.

Why then do we observe people arguing for the program on the grounds that it will help the poor? The answer, I think, is fairly simple. Most of us like to think of ourselves as helping the poor and doing other good things, and we like also to have our own income and real well-being improved. The politician who argues that you should do something which will benefit you, not because it will benefit you but because it is abstractly good and just, gets more votes than the politician who points out the difficulties with that line of reasoning. All of us like to think that we are better, more altruistic, more charitable, than we actually are. But although we have this desire, we don't want to pay for it. We are willing to make a sacrifice of perhaps 5 percent of our real income, in charitable aid to others. We would like to think of ourselves, however, as making much larger transfers without actually making them. One of the functions of the politician in our society is to meet this demand — the demand I suppose one can call a demand for hypocrisy but nevertheless a very human demand. He provides arguments that programs which benefit us personally are actually aimed at helping the poor, the national interest, cure of cancer, etc.

Note that I am not criticizing people who have these particular motives. I have them myself. And the "well-intentioned" cover for programs whose actual motives are mainly selfish is endemic not only in democratic politics but in politics everywhere. We also find it in the market. The businessman, changing his product line to make more money, is apt to refer to the change as "serving the customer." In fact, if he makes more money he probably will, but his motives are somewhat more crass.

Bismarck obviously knew of this and he was one of the more successful politicians of modern times. The changes he made in Germany when he invented what we now call the welfare state both directly benefit a large group of people and could be argued for on charitable grounds. That political trick has continued.

That the proponents of most generalized plans are not really particularly interested in helping the poor seems to me fairly certain, mainly because in reading their works I never find discussions of the actual probability that their programs will hurt the poor. In general, as I demonstrated above, the program can be altered in such a way that it does not hurt the poor, but that is never part of the real-life political proposal. From this, I deduce that the actual motive of most of these generalization programs is not to help the poor but to help people who are well above the poor level.

Once again, I am not criticizing people for trying to benefit themselves through use of the political process. We all do it, some more successfully than others. What I am saying is that we should have intellectual clarity in dealing with these problems. We may not particularly want to help the poor, but if we do want to help the poor the effective methods, in general, are means-tested, direct-aid programs. Free medical aid for the poor, pensions for the elderly poor, college scholarships for the children of the poor (probably with arrangements so that if the children of the poor later become wealthy they will repay the state for this investment) — all are better ways of helping the poor than general programs which provide services to everyone.

The point of this chapter has been that means-tested, direct aid for the poor, rather than the Bismarckian generalization of programs for everyone, is more likely to help the poor, if that be the objective. As I said at the beginning, this seems obvious and it is hard to see why people argue on the other side, but the fact remains they do.

IV.
Old-Age Pensions

In the United States, we have not adopted the whole of Bismarck's program, but we have adopted one major part of it. Our Social Security System is a modification of a Bismarckian scheme.

The reader has no doubt heard a great deal about the current crisis in the Social Security System and the demographic factors which make it likely the crisis will become worse. I don't wish to quarrel with any of this. It is not my main topic. I assume that people interested in that aspect of the matter can get information quite readily from other sources.[13]

Let me begin by discussing the Social Security System while largely ignoring its effects on the poor. We will then turn to its effects on the poor in the latter part of the chapter. As we shall see, basically the Social Security System is a massive program transferring funds from one part of the population to another, almost but not quite, regardless of their respective wealth.

But before dealing with this formally, I must digress briefly to discuss one of Prince Bismarck's more brilliant political ideas. It occurred to him that if it were announced that part of the cost of the social security system was paid by the employee, and part by his employer, then it would appear

[13]There is one aspect of the demographic problem that is seldom mentioned. In recent years, the life expectancy of older people, i.e., people over 65, has been rising very rapidly. It is not clear what caused this rise, but in any event it could, of course, have disastrous financial effects on the Social Security Administration.

to the employee to be cheaper than it actually was. In fact, I do not believe there are any economists who doubt that the whole social security tax, employer's and employee's share, is paid by the employee in the sense that his salary is that much lower than it otherwise would be. Bismarck realized, however, that this could be concealed.

Note the cleverness of Bismarck's idea. If he had put the tax entirely on the employer, then the well-established economic proposition that a payroll tax was actually paid by the worker, not by the employer, would have been brought into play. By splitting it into two parts, as we do, this is concealed and a great many workers no doubt think that they are paying half as much for their social security pension as they in fact are paying. I hope none of the readers of this book will be so deceived.

But let us now look at the whole problem with a little formality. I am going to simplify it a great deal, of course, but the basic propositions will be standard. My simplification will be based upon one invented by Paul Samuelson.

Suppose that we are in a nation which has had a social security system running, substantially unchanged for a long time — long enough so that when the people now receiving pensions, 60 or 70 years ago first entered the employment market, the system was substantially identical to what it is now. This is, of course, not true of any real world social security system — not even Bismarck's own German program, which is now more than 100 years old, because the system has been sharply changed over time. But we will deal with these changes later.

Let us further assume that the social security system works a little differently from the way we think of it working now. Let's assume each individual entering the social security system was compelled to pay a tax of 10 percent of his wage. We compute the share of the total wage bill in each year that he had paid in. Let us say that he had paid in 1/10,000,000th of the wage bill in a given year. Over his active employment life these shares are added up so that when he retires at 65 he has paid in a total amount which is 45/10,000,000ths of the total wage bill. Note that the amount that he would pay in each year would be different because the total wages are growing. One 10,000,000th of a wage bill in 1980 is quite a bit greater than 1/10,000,000th in 1935. As we will see below this fact is vital to the success of the system.

When he retires he receives a pension which is actuarially calculated not in dollars but in terms of share of the wage bill. Let us suppose, for example, that if he had paid in 45/10,000,000ths of the total wage bill, then it is actuarially likely that he will live another 15 years and, hence, we can pay him 3/10,000,000ths of the total wage bill each year for the next 15 years.

All of this may seem mysterious because you will note there is no accumulation of funds at interest. Nevertheless, it is more or less the way social security systems in fact work. No money is accumulated and invested at interest, but the individuals who are paid in 1983 are, in fact, receiving payment which is raised by a tax on wages, i.e., is a particular share of wages. We will talk about the alternative, a true investment, in a moment. The social security system invented by Bismarck does not involve any such investment. It involves a tax on an individual during his working life to be repaid from a tax on other individuals when he retires. Our share of the total wage bill is more or less, not exactly but generally, the way this works out.

Looked at from the standpoint of a man who has lived his life under this system, was it a good bargain or not? You will note that at the moment there is nothing in this program that in any way helps, or for that matter injures the poor. It simply redistributes a person's income from one part of his life to another, together with paying him additional money proportional to the growth of the total payroll.

Whether the man gained depends on the rate of interest. If the rate of interest was higher than the rate of growth of the total payroll, the individual would have been better off if he had saved the same amount of money and invested it rather than being part of the social security program. If the rate of growth of the payroll is greater than the rate of interest, however, the reverse would be true.

It should be said here that there is another effect. Presumably, if everyone had been saving money and investing it, the total capital in society would have been greater and, hence, the rate of growth in society would have been greater. I regret to say that although this seems theoretically clear, statistical investigations have not produced unambiguous evidence that it has occurred.

But leaving that much-disputed point aside, let us briefly think about the comparison of the interest rate and the rate of growth of the wage bill. The period of the social security in both the United States and Germany, and for that matter all the other countries that have adopted it, has been one of considerable instability. Both the interest rate and the rate of growth of the total wage bill have fluctuated sharply. There is no obvious reason to believe they will stop so fluctuating in the near future. Nevertheless, it seems a reasonable proposition that, as a norm, the interest rate will be higher than the rate of growth of the wage bill. At the moment it is much larger. On the other hand, there have been periods in the recent past when, due to unanticipated inflation, the return on interest has been lower than the rate of growth of total wages. I believe, however, that the general situation is that the interest rate will be higher than the rate of growth of the wage bill.

If this is so, then if we look at this stable system which has been in existence for a long time, everyone loses under it. They would all have been better off if at the time they started into the system they had instead invested their money in some kind of a private insurance system.[14] It does not follow, however, that it would be sensible for the people in this system to decide to dismantle it. Suppose, for example, that we just stopped paying the pension and told everybody to

[14]Better yet, into a number of different investment schemes. Never put all your eggs in one basket.

save. Obviously, the older people would be badly damaged. The younger people however, would gain.

Assume, for example, some person is just entering the system and that the predicted rate of growth of the payroll is 3 percent a year and the predicted standard interest rate is 5 percent. He could either save less than 10 percent and have the same pension when he retires or save 10 percent and have a larger pension upon retirement. If we just cancelled the system, he would gain. The person who has already paid in for one year would also gain, although less. Each additional year the person would gain less and less for the change. Eventually we would reach a changeover point which, with the numbers I have just given, would be about the age of 40. From then on the cancelling of the system would injure everyone more than they would benefit, because the accumulated pension rights that would be sacrificed in cancelling the system would be worth more to that point than the interest they would receive on their future savings.

At first glance it would appear there is another way out; i.e., we can continue taxing people, pay off the existing liabilities but not accumulate new ones. This would be a very desirable system from the standpoint of all of the older people, but it would mean that the younger people pay a heavy tax over their lives and receive nothing in return. There doesn't seem to be any way out. The system is worse for everyone than the alternative of saving money and investing it. The transition from the present stable state to a system in which everyone saved would be extremely painful for a large part of the population, although which part would depend to some extent on the exact details of the change method.

But as we mentioned before, no country has really gotten into the fully stable, long-run equilibrium of the system.

Let us now consider the starting up period. What happens when you first establish a social security system? For simplicity, assume that it is established full-grown — that is, at one point in time we begin collecting taxes and paying out pensions, with the taxes being collected from everyone under

65 and the pensions going to all people over 65. (This was not the way the system was actually developed. Normally, when the system is set up, and for that matter when it is extended to a new group, there is a short period during which taxes are collected and no pension payments are made. For example, from 1937 to 1940, the tax was collected and except for a few extraordinary circumstances no one received pensions. But for simplicity we will ignore this detail.)

The first thing to be said is that we have the reverse of the effect which we have when the system is dismantled. The younger people who would be better off saving and putting their money into some kind of investment where it would earn interest will be injured by the establishment of the system and older people will gain. Further, the gain for the older people will be much larger than the loss to the younger people who are old enough to vote. Much of the gain for people over the age of 40 will be paid not by the people between the age of 18 and 40 but those under 18 and the unborn.

Thus, consider someone who is now 41 and who will retire at the age of 65. When he retires at the age of 65, people who are slightly too young to vote now will be 41 years old. Those born in the year after the program is inaugurated will be 24. Both will be paying taxes to support the retiree. And in both cases they will in fact have already been paying full social security tax during the whole of their employed lives.

Our 41-year-old man will, of course, pay taxes himself from the beginning of the program to age 65. If we assume, as we assumed above, that the rate of growth of the total national wage bill is 3 percent and interest rate is 5 percent, he will only be slightly better off than he would have been had he saved his tax contributions and invested them. In general, all of the people younger than he will be worse off as a result of the scheme. How much worse off depends on how much younger than he they are. People older than he will make profits; once again the older they are the more profits they will make.

No system has ever been introduced exactly in this way.

Normally, there is some accumulation period before pensions begin to be paid, but this is characteristically much less than what is needed to fund the pensions. Further, the extension of the system normally functions for the people to whom it is extended much like the introduction of a brand new system would. Last, but by no means least, increases in the system paid for by increases in the tax base are, in essence, equivalent to setting up a new small system added onto the previous ones. They therefore do have the effect described.

Thus, we can see that essentially the Social Security System is a simple transfer from the young to the old. This does not, of course, indicate that it is undesirable, but it does indicate that it doesn't necessarily help the poor. It is true that, on the whole, older people have lower incomes than younger people, a fact which is to a considerable extent offset by the ownership of fully paid-for houses by 60 percent of all families over 65. The difference is not gigantic. If we were interested in helping the poor, we would extend our aid only to the elderly poor and not to all elderly.

But now let us consider the minor aspect of the system — its effect on poverty. For this purpose I would like to distinguish between the system during most of its life, i.e., up to the 1977 amendments to the Act, and the system since 1977, which is the system we have now. The reason I am giving so much emphasis to the pre-1977 version is a political judgment on my part. I believe that the pre-1977 system comes closer to representing the political equilibrium than the post-1977 system. It is my opinion that the amendments of 1977 greatly weakened the political support of the Act and that it is likely that they must be reversed if the system is to be kept viable. This is a political not an economic judgment.

Turning then to the pre-1977 system, if we just consider the Social Security System and nothing else, it apparently was mildly anti-poor. It transferred a certain amount of money from the poor to the upper income groups. An interesting characteristic of the system is that I have to say "apparently." No one has actually worked out in detail the net effect the complicated provisions of the Act have on people in the various income brackets. Some of them benefit the well-off and some of them benefit the poor. The best study I am aware of considers all the provisions except the ferocious discrimination against working wives and comes to the conclusion that, on the whole, the system is roughly proportional, i.e., the poor get back about as much on their payment as the well-off.

If, however, we add the severe discrimination against working wives we should consider that when the program was first inaugurated in 1937 almost all working wives came from poor families. It is still true today that there are far more working wives in the lower income groups than in the upper. It seems almost certain that the net effect of the program up to 1977 was a modest transfer away from the poor towards the middle classes. This transfer took place not because the poor were poor but because the system discriminated against working wives and more of them are poor.

But if we look at the Social Security System more broadly, i.e., consider it as part of the total income redistribution system in the United States, then it clearly discriminates against the poor. As a matter of fact, it was intended to injure the poor. This sound like a harsh judgment, but I don't think anyone who looks at history, or for that matter the current discussion of it, can avoid that conclusion. Once we realize that the elderly poor were being taken care of by other programs at the time Social Security was put into effect and would be taken care of today by other programs if Social Security did not exist, it is obvious.

One of the original arguments for the establishment of Social Security, and still one of the arguments that its proponents use, is that there are many people in society who are poor and either cannot, or in some cases through improvidence do not, save money for their old age. We are then compelled to take care of them ourselves through the various programs that exist. Hence, it is desirable to, in essence, force them to save. In other words, we begin with a situation in which there is a general tax on the population as a whole to help the poor in their old age, and convert this into a situation in which the poor, during the whole of their lives, are to at least some extent taxed to take care of themselves in their old age. Clearly, the poor are worse off in the second situation than the first, and the upper income groups are better off. Since we have never given a great deal to the poor, even the elderly poor, the change is not great but it is real, and it is an anti-poor change.

Consider the situation of an old, poor man who has been poor all his life. He always had a fairly low income and had to pay substantial Social Security tax out of that income. Now that he is old he receives a Social Security pension, but a small one because of the small earnings throughout his life. Society does not want him to live on that small pension and so he receives additional payments under whatever program happens to be current at that time. It would have been poor relief in 1937 and today is Supplemental Security Income. But note that his total income will be about the same whether he has a Social Security pension or not. In other words, he has gained nothing at all in his old age from all of those tax payments. He has the same income he would have had he not made them. The rest of society, however, has gained because they have collected those taxes.

Once again, I find that when I talk to people about the Social Security System, one of the major arguments offered for its retention is that lots of poor people would not, or could not, save money for their old age and we would have to support them anyway, so the system compels them to pay. In a way, this is a moral argument: it is morally right for people to provide for their old age even if we have to compel them to. I don't want to quarrel with this value judgment, but I do think it should be kept clearly in mind that it does not help the poor financially whatever it may do for their moral state.

Now let us turn to the 1977 amendments which considerably changed the income distribution effect of the system. First, the poor are in the same situation as before.

They will pay taxes all of their lives and will receive a pension when they are old. This pension will, in essence, simply be subtracted from a payment which they receive for being poor and elderly. In essence, they pay an additional tax but end up with the same income they would have if they didn't pay it.

If we look at the rest of the distribution of income, however, there has been a distinct equalizing change in the payments. The tax has been extended to higher income brackets, with the result that it is not as regressive as it used to be, and the repayment ratio, i.e., how much a person gets back, has been changed in a sharply progressive manner. There aren't any detailed calculations that I know of, but as a rough rule of thumb the bottom 60 percent of the population gains from this change and the top 40 percent is injured. Of course, the bottom 60 percent includes the poor, who in fact make no gains at all for the reasons given above. But if we take people who have during their lives accumulated enough Social Security pension rights and other wealth that they are not eligible for Supplemental Security Income, then those who are in the bottom 60 percent of the population probably gain by the readjustment. The program has become less an insurance program and more an income redistribution program.

In my opinion this scheme is politically unstable, and indeed, I believe one of the reasons Social Security is in so much trouble now is that it has been changed so that many more people are injured by it than before. In any event, the current system of Social Security as contrasted to the previous system leaves the true poor in the same situation they were in before. That is, they are basically dependent on other programs to supplement the Social Security program. The lower income classes who cannot really be called poor, benefit, and the upper income classes, which in this case does not mean only the wealthy but also the middle class, are injured.

To sum up, the Social Security program is essentially a transfer to the older part of the population from the younger part of the population. When it was started its political advantages were obvious, since many of the younger population were too young to vote. There is no doubt that was what attracted Bismarck. Once established, dismantling it will injure a great many people. There are obvious ethical arguments about the majority of the people who have paid Social Security payments most of their lives being entitled to a pension. It should, of course, be said that there probably is no single American today drawing a pension for whom tax payments fully justifies the present pension. The system has been expanded fairly rapidly and continuously, with the result that most people are still in what we may call the new part of the system, i.e., they receive considerably more than they put in. In the long-run stable situation this will no longer be true.

V.
Helping the Poor vs. Helping the Well-Organized

Discussion of government income redistribution usually turns on the problem of whether we should try to equalize incomes. I hope that I have convinced the reader by now that this is only a minor aspect of the problem. Most government income redistribution goes not to the poor but to people who for one reason or another have sufficient political influence to get it. The poor are normally not among this group although they certainly do receive considerable amounts of funds from the government, probably mainly because people are charitable.

Why the basic discussion has tended to deal only with helping the poor is not clear. Let me go back to a piece of not-so-ancient history: the gasoline price controls which were installed after the organization of the oil cartel in 1973. The average person remembers this as a period in which the newspapers denounced the large oil companies and in which he had to spend long periods of time in gasoline lines. He may also remember that gasoline prices were lower then than they are now although, interestingly, if you allow for inflation they were not very much lower.

Let us look at this as a political example of redistribution. It was talked about at the time as something which was necessary to prevent the poor from having to pay too high prices for their gasoline. In a way it was slightly pro-poor because the time of the poor is worth less than the time of other people and, hence, sitting in gas lines was less costly to them than it was to others. Indeed, some of the poor actually got jobs[15] taking other peoples' cars through gas lines. But this was a minor effect.

What then were the major effects of price controls other than long gas lines? The price controls held the price of gasoline at a low enough price that one could not have imported Arab oil at the cartel price and sold it. There was a control on the wellhead price of American oil which was kept much below the Arab price. This would have meant that those American oil companies with a lot of domestic capacity would have made a lot of money, and those that did not have domestic capacity would have gone bankrupt if nothing else had been done. The government, therefore, set up an elaborate scheme under which, in essence, domestic oil well owners were required to subsidize the import of oil from the Arabs. Sending in the Marines is no longer fashionable and the only price, therefore, that could be kept down was the American oil well price.[16]

What were the results? First, American car owners bought gasoline at a lower price than they otherwise would have. Of course, they had to sit in lines, and that is a costly activity. It seems likely, however, that the average driver benefited in net, even if not much, from the combination of lower prices and long gas lines. This gain presumably was roughly proportional to the amount of gasoline consumed, which means, of course, that it was to some extent larger for upper income people than for lower income people.

The other big gainers here were those extremely wealthy people, the Arab Sheikhs. Without the subsidy for imported oil, the amounts purchased by the United States would have fallen off considerably. This was, of course, the program that was implemented in Europe. I made some calculations on this, based on the existing data on elasticity, and concluded

[15]Which they did not report to their relief supervisor.

[16]I am simplifying this system. Some of my readers may think oversimplifying, but the full details are too lengthy to elaborate here.

that for every dollar saved by American gasoline consumers the members of OPEC made an additional two dollars. Of course, the domestic consumer had a good deal of the dollar he saved offset by having to sit in gas lines and rearrange his life to meet the shortage. (It is possible that if the United States had not put on the price controls the drop in demand for Arab oil would have been large enough that the cartel would have collapsed. The last is only a possibility, but we should not have been offering the Arabs a guarantee against the risk of breaking their cartel even if that risk was not gigantic.)

Here, then, we see a program which was argued for in terms of helping the poor and which helped them only slightly if at all. It did help almost all Americans who didn't own oil wells, although the help was probably modest. There was a very large gain from the program for a group of people who most Americans don't think are particularly meritorious and certainly are not poor, the Arab Sheikhs.

I should say that there is no evidence whatsoever that the Arabs lobbied for the program. They apparently did not understand it either. Indeed, it is astonishing that ever since the original cartel the American government has carried out a number of policies which indirectly tend to stabilize the cartel. As far as I know, in no case has Arab political influence been behind these policies. They are usually intended for something else and just accidently benefit the cartel. They have, however, cost the American taxpayer and gasoline purchaser a great deal of money.

My point here has been that a good many programs which purport to help the poor actually do not, and "helping the poor" is in a way simply a cover for other motives. Clearly, the American voter who talked about the need to keep price controls on gasoline to help the poor was primarily concerned with price controls to help himself. He did not understand economics enough to realize that this was not a good way of helping himself, even though that was his objective. The aid to the poor was a political cover story.

We find this commonly in the redistribution which goes

on in our society. A great many programs purport to be aimed at helping the poor, but actually are aimed at helping someone else — someone who is politically more influential. It should be said, of course, that there are programs that do help the poor, and some of the programs which actually aim at benefiting the upper middle class have as a by-product some aid to the poor.

But, many government programs which are announced in terms of helping the poor simply injure them. Most of our agricultural programs make food more expensive, and these programs tend to concentrate on the types of foods that the poor consume. Luxury foods are seldom produced under acreage restrictions, but wheat is.

What I am suggesting, then, is that the basic argument on income redistribution has been miscast. One can be interested in helping the poor and against our present income redistribution policies.[17] On the other hand, one can be interested in getting some special government benefit and totally uninterested in the poor.

This is the reason, I suspect, why the means-tested programs are unpopular now. They help the poor and no one else. The politically powerful groups who would like to use the government to increase their wealth cannot generally benefit from means-tested programs. But if we want to help the poor, that's the way to go.

How did we get into this situation? Most people learn in their high school civics courses that the government exists to serve the public interest and to equalize incomes. It should be frankly said that as a matter of fact the government does many things which serve the public interest, and it is quite possible to argue that it also equalizes income. Furthermore, if we look through history, most governments have done some things to benefit the public interest, maintaining police and defense forces, building roads, etc., and have put heavy taxes on those wealthy people who are not government of-

[17]When I say "our" here, I really mean the whole civilized world, not just the United States. Our programs are very similar to those in other countries.

ficials while making charitable gifts to the poor. They still do so today.

Throughout history, however, governments have also been used as a means of increasing the wealth of people who are by no means poor. The various royal palaces scattered across Europe are evidence that at least one group of wealthy people found the government a source of more wealth. But the kings and noblemen who lived in those palaces were not the only people who used the government to augment their wealth. From earliest times, governments have been used as a source of revenue. We should not be surprised about this. Most human beings are interested in improving their incomes and are willing to use a wide variety of methods to do so. If I can raise my income by lobbying in Congress for something or other, I will do so.

This whole subject — the use of the government as a way of increasing wealth — was rather ignored by social scientists for the last century. Recently, a great deal of interest, particularly among economists, has been focused on the problem. It has the undescriptive title of "rent-seeking."[18] Lurking behind this poor title is simply the study of the way in which the government is used to raise people's income.

The subject of this study is complicated in detail, but its general lines are simple and indeed many of my readers may regard them as obvious. I would not quarrel with the view that the main outlines are obvious, only point out that they are not normally talked about in discussions of income redistribution. Normally, it is discussed in terms of helping the poor and not in terms of helping those who want to be helped.

In a democracy, the way it works is fairly simple and straightforward. A great many, probably most, voters tend to vote in terms of what they think will benefit them. The Tombigbee Canal, for example, will indeed benefit people living

[18]See "Towards A Theory of the Rent-Seeking Society," edited by James M. Buchanan, Robert D. Tollison, and Gordon Tullock, Texas A&M Press, 1981, for a collection of articles on the topic.

along its course, mainly because its construction activity will raise their wealth and not because of the canal itself. We should expect them and the political representatives they have in Washington to favor it. Similarly, farmers benefit from our farm program and vote for people who favor it.

We do not want to oversimplify here. Most of the residents along the Tombigbee, and most farmers, are not solely interested in their own wealth, but they are interested in it. Thus, most people running for Congress talk about the public good, helping the poor, etc., but also give great emphasis to various things which they know will directly benefit special interest groups in their constituency.

Once a matter has reached Congress, various bills dealing with the special interests are passed by a combination of logrolling and lobbying. Logrolling, in which congressmen trade votes on issues, is the foundation of democratic politics, although not discussed much in the high school civics courses. Lobbying is also important, not only in democratic politics but in all other kinds of politics that we know of. It does get discussed in high school civic classes, mainly being denounced as wicked.

I don't wish to quarrel with anyone who believes lobbying is wicked, but I should point out that we can hardly expect people to stop doing it as long as it is profitable to the lobbyist. If we organize ourselves and hire a lobbyist, and he tells congressmen that we are going to vote the next election in terms of how successfully the congressmen get our interests supported, we can expect that the congressmen will make a good college try and that we will get a reasonable return on our resources. Looked at from the standpoint of the person contributing to the lobby or voting in favor of his special interests, the situation is just like any other investment or act intended to increase his income. This is what is called "rent-seeking," and it is an unfortunate characteristic of our modern society that this is immensely important.

If we look over the world's history we find most of the time that this kind of rent-seeking has been immensely important. During a period in the 19th Century it was relatively unimportant. It was not that the governments did not engage in rent-seeking, but they were small enough that rent-seeking was a rather small percentage of the gross national product. By now, the second half of the 20th Century, governments all over the world have gone back to the historic norm. They are once more quite large and once more rent-seeking has become a large percentage of the G.N.P.

Rent-seeking is economically important, not because the various special interest groups distort the economy, although this does occur, but because the resources invested in attempting to obtain these special privileges could have been invested in more productive activities. Rent-seeking and the use of government to obtain wealth is, from the standpoint of society as a whole, a completely wasteful activity. Somebody gains and somebody loses. Further, it is always true that the person who loses loses much more than the person who gains. This is different from the market activity where the gain of Mr. A may lead to no loss but a gain to all other members of society. If it does lead to a loss of other members of society, then those losses will be smaller than Mr. A's gain, so that there is a net gain for society as a whole.[19]

To a considerable extent, income redistribution is the result of rent-seekng. To a considerable extent, however, it is rationalized in terms of helping the poor even if it doesn't. The reason for this apparently is simply that information conditions in politics are poor.

Once again, we are turning to an area which, for many generations, was largely ignored by social scientists but has now become quite important. This is the economics of information. Scholars of this area study the question of whether people will acquire information or won't, usually with the assumption that they only acquire information which is worth as much to them as the cost of getting it. This assump-

[19]I am simplifying fairly drastically here. In particular, there are, of course, the cases where there are large externalities in which the market does not work. Fortunately, these do not seem to be overwhelmingly common.

tion is a simplifying one. All of us have a good deal of information we have acquired because we were simply interested in it or we thought we had a duty to acquire it. If the system is to operate well, however, we should have more information.

The basic problem with democratic politics is that, for most voters, acquiring politically relevant information is not worth more than it costs. Consider, for example, a citizen voter who during the time of the first establishment of the oil cartel, 1973-74, decided that he would become well-informed about the actual effect of the price controls in the United States. The average citizen is not accustomed to doing that kind of research, is not familiar with the type of libraries which carry the data, and doesn't have the necessary training to understand a good deal of the material he would find if he looked. If he actually wanted to be well-informed, he would have to put a great deal of time and effort into studying the problem.

But once he had become well-informed what effect would it have? The only result would be that he could cast an informed vote in the next election and perhaps write a letter to his congressman. The payoff to him in the sense of changing American policy would be so small as to be quite invisible. Thus, he would have spent a great deal of time and energy in searching for information which actually did not benefit him. He would have raised his income considerably more had he looked for some information directly concerning his private business.

This line of reasoning frequently makes people indignant. The argument that we all have a duty to be well-informed is repeated frequently by teachers and preachers. I do not want to quarrel with it. I simply would point out that most people do not have any material motive for becoming well-informed about politics. They do know something about politics because they find it an interesting topic. As far as we can tell, however, their knowledge of politics tends to be rather superficial and concentrated on exciting rather than important matters. Public opinion polls invariably show the voters are badly informed about complex topics. Since the bulk of income redistribution matters are complex, they are badly informed about them.

Here it should be said that the special interest groups normally have an interest in diminishing the information of the average voter. If they can sell him some false tale which supports their particular effort to rob the treasury, it pays. They have resources and normally make efforts to produce this kind of misinformation. But that would not work if the voter had a strong motive to learn the truth. There is not much point in trying to convince housewives that the canned tomatoes you are selling are much better quality than they are. She may buy one can but as soon as she opens it she finds it is of low quality and doesn't go back. In politics, unfortunately, this rule does not exist, because the voter never has the opportunity to open the can.

The problem, then, appears to be a serious one. The government, in addition to generating various public goods and to some extent helping the poor, is being used to a large extent to transfer income back and forth in our society in a highly wasteful manner. Further, if we look over history, this has been a characteristic role of government throughout almost all of recorded time. It is true that the 19th and early 20th Centuries, in the area around the North Atlantic Ocean, this activity was rather minor, but that was the historical exception. The normal fate is a rent-seeking government.

What can we do? We should turn to the experience of the 19th Century, the great exception. In England from about 1775 to about 1850, a general climate of opinion was built up under which the government was confined to those activities which it could actually perform reasonably well. This climate of opinion developed partly as the result of clear and unrelenting propaganda by the people who understood the problem and who were interested in benefiting both themselves and the country. This was a period in which a large number of intellectuals argued not for larger slices of the pie but for a larger pie.

Unfortunately, the situation changed. Today the government is engaged in many activities, most of which are rationalized either in terms of improving the national product or helping the poor. In fact, the government's major activity is redistribution.

What is needed today to curb government overextension is to duplicate the intellectual accomplishments of the early 19th Century. Voters must be given accurate information about the true nature, purposes and effects of government redistribution programs as they affect them. Without it, they will remain unable to evaluate redistribution on the basis of actual results rather than alleged intentions, and unable to know if they really want to pay the price.

The proponents of redistribution claim that their programs help the poor. They do help the poor — which they also help to create — but not much. Basically, the modern redistributive state transfers money back and forth within the middle class based on the power of political organization and public misinformation. This political power is not easily overcome, but we should see to it that the truth is known. Until it is, the government will continue to serve the interests of political factions in the middle class, using money appropriated under the guise of helping the poor.